TIMELESS POPULAR CLASSICS

40 Piano Arrangements of the Most-Requested Favorites

ARRANGED BY DAN COATES

This collection offers accessible piano arrangements of timeless, popular songs. It contains 40 favorites that are instantly familiar and motivating to learn. Pianists will enjoy the jazzy harmonies of "As Time Goes By," the powerful climax of "Bridge over Troubled Water," the driving rhythms of "Don't Stop Believin'," the iconic hook of "Colors of the Wind," and the triumphant fanfare of the *Star Wars* theme—page after page of great music!

Arranged by prolific popular-music arranger Dan Coates, each piece is not only fun to play but also quality teaching material that can help improve sight-reading ability while reinforcing essential piano-playing skills. Students can become familiar with a variety of root-position and inverted chords while learning "Embraceable You" or master syncopations by practicing "I Got Rhythm." "If I Only Had a Brain" provides an opportunity to learn a piece with swung eighth notes, and "My Funny Valentine" can be used to explore the keys of C minor and E-flat major. Each arrangement is edited with helpful fingering and pedaling indications to aid learning. Enjoy these *Timeless Popular Classics*!

Contents

GERSHWIN® and GEORGE GERSHWIN® are registered trademarks of Gershwin Enterprises.
IRA GERSHWIN™ is a trademark of Gershwin Enterprises.

Produced by
Alfred Music
P.O. Box 10003
Van Nuys, CA 91410-0003
alfred.com

Printed in USA.

ISBN-10: 1-4706-3503-8
ISBN-13: 978-1-4706-3503-9

Cover Photo
Piano: © Getty Images / peterhung101

As Time Goes By

(from *Casablanca*)

Words and Music by Herman Hupfeld
Arr. Dan Coates

Moderately, with expression

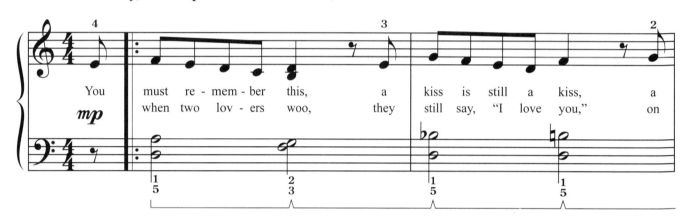

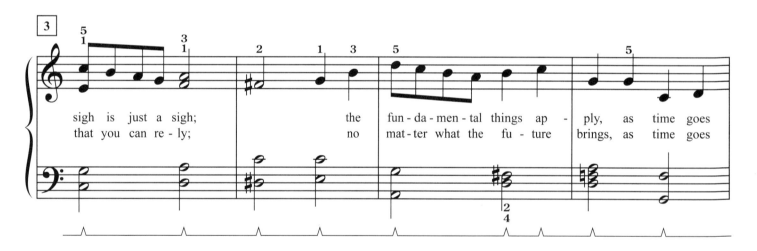

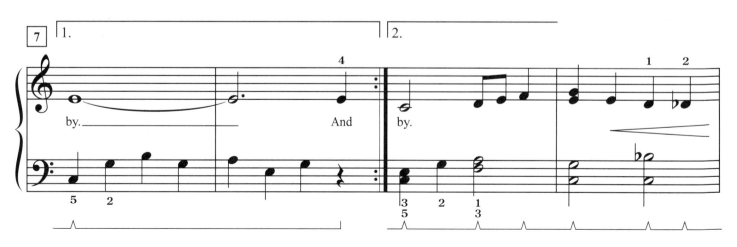

At Last

Music by Harry Warren
Lyrics by Mack Gordon
Arr. Dan Coates

Slowly, with feeling

My heart was wrapped in clo - ver the night I looked at

you. I found a dream that I can

speak to, a dream that I can call my own. I found a

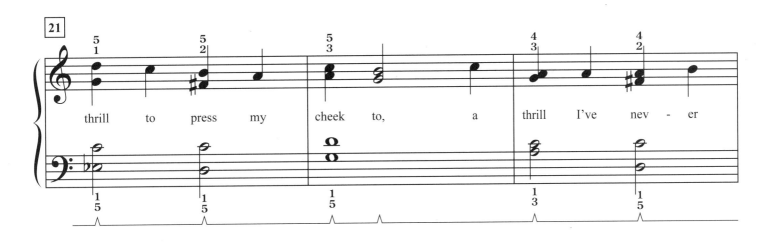

thrill to press my cheek to, a thrill I've nev - er

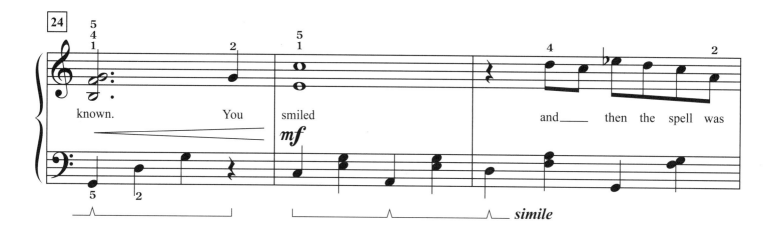

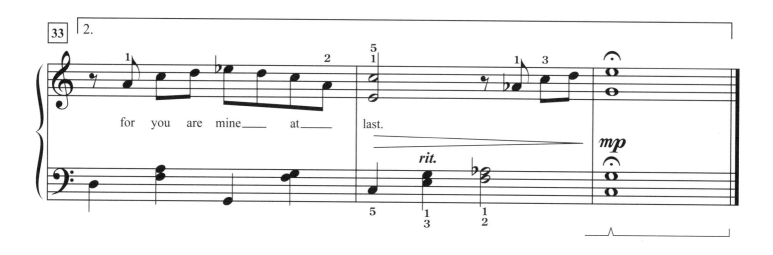

Beauty and the Beast

(from Walt Disney's *Beauty and the Beast*)

Lyrics by Howard Ashman
Music by Alan Menken
Arr. Dan Coates

Slowly, with expression

Bridge over Troubled Water

Words and Music by Paul Simon
Arr. Dan Coates

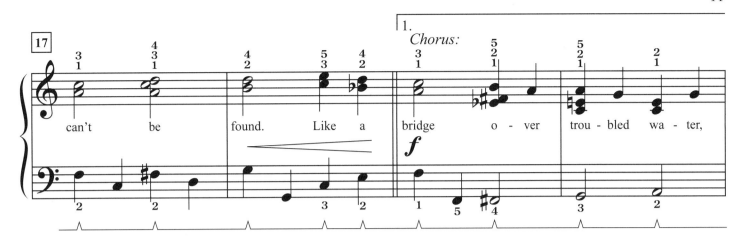

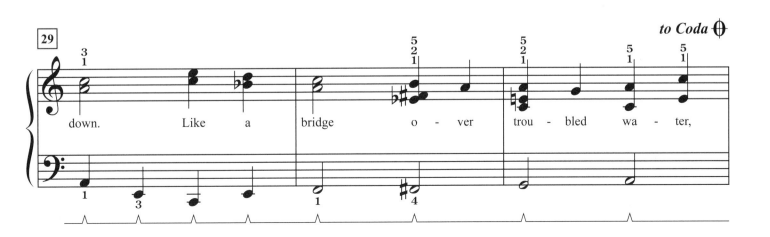

Verse 2:
When you're down and out,
When you're on the street,
When evening falls so hard, I will comfort you.
I'll take your part when darkness comes
And pain is all around.
Like a bridge over troubled water, I will lay me down.
Like a bridge over troubled water, I will lay me down.

Verse 3:
Sail on, silver girl, sail on by.
Your time has come to shine,
All your dreams are on their way.
See how they shine, if you need a friend.
I'm sailing right behind.
Like a bridge over troubled water, I will ease your mind.
Like a bridge over troubled water, I will ease your mind.

Blue Moon

Music by Richard Rodgers
Lyrics by Lorenz Hart
Arr. Dan Coates

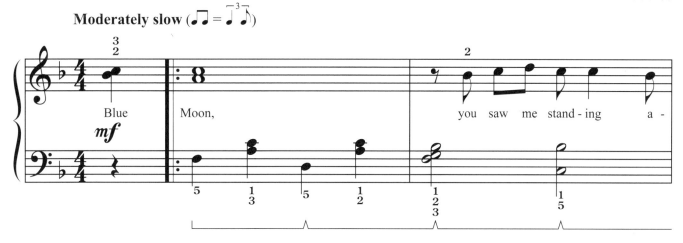

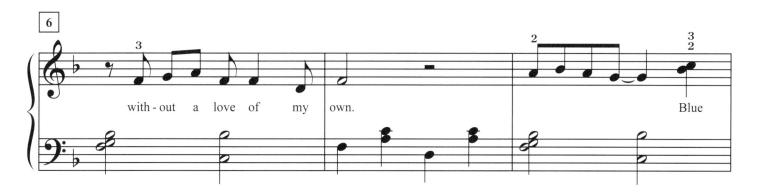

Moon, you knew just what I was there for.

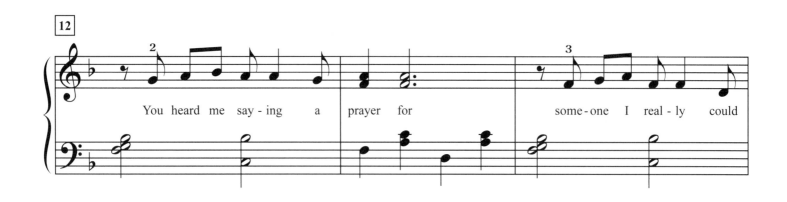

You heard me say - ing a prayer for some - one I real - ly could

care for. _____ And then there sud - den - ly ap - peared be -

fore me the on - ly one my arms will ev - er hold. I heard some -

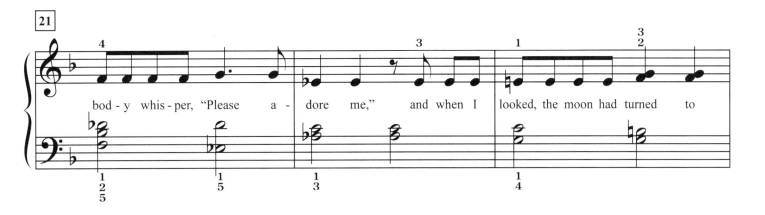

bod - y whis - per, "Please a - dore me," and when I looked, the moon had turned to

gold! Blue Moon, now I'm no long - er a - lone

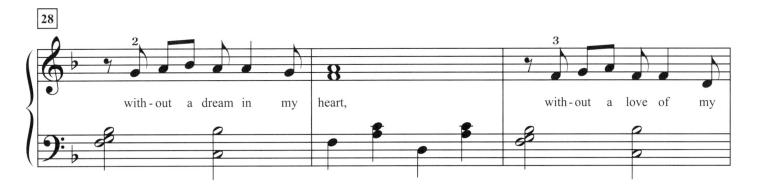

with - out a dream in my heart, with - out a love of my

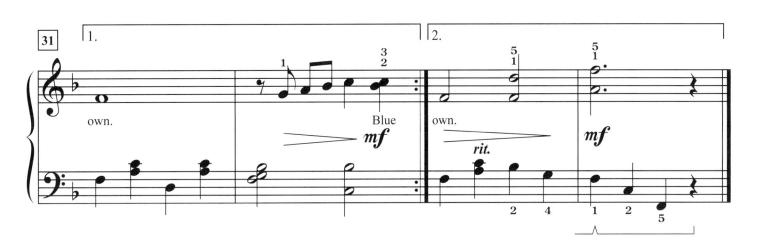

own. Blue own.

But Not for Me

Music and Lyrics by
George Gershwin and Ira Gershwin
Arr. Dan Coates

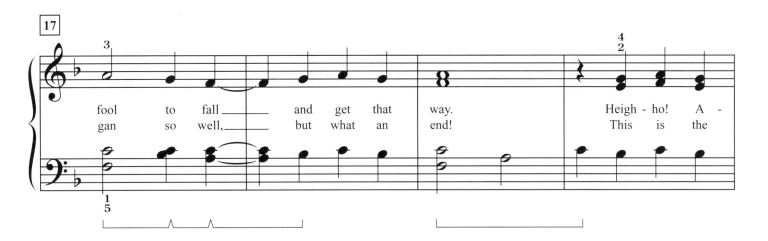

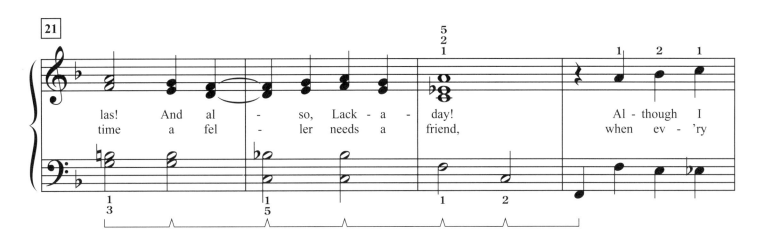

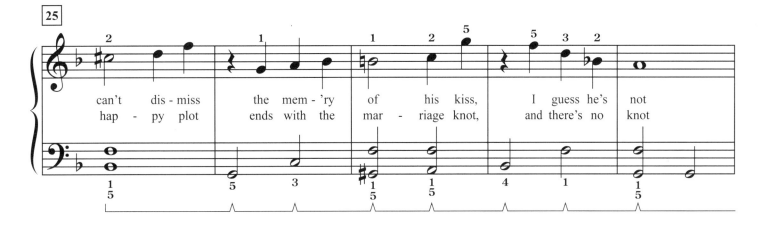

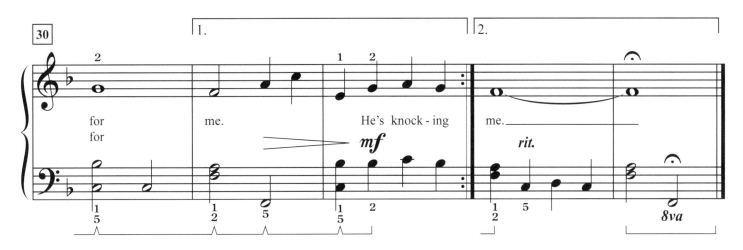

Can You Feel the Love Tonight

(from Walt Disney's *The Lion King*)

Music by Elton John
Words by Tim Rice
Arr. Dan Coates

Colors of the Wind

(from Walt Disney's *Pocahontas*)

Lyrics by Stephen Schwartz
Music by Alan Menken
Arr. Dan Coates

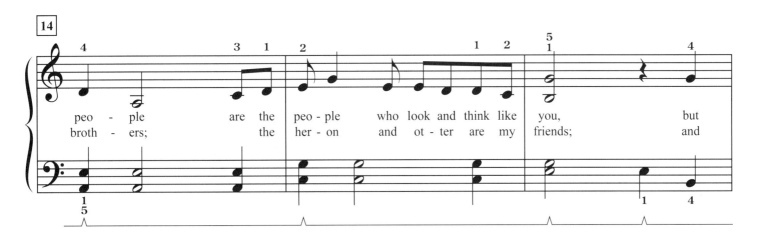

peo - ple   are the peo - ple   who look and think like you,   but
broth - ers;   the her - on   and ot - ter are my friends;   and

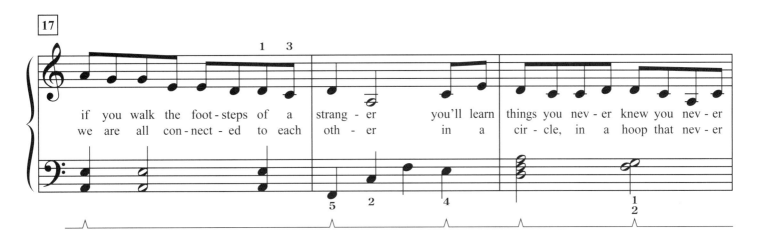

if you walk the foot-steps of a   strang - er   you'll learn things you nev-er knew you nev-er
we are all con-nect-ed to each oth - er   in a   cir-cle, in a hoop that nev-er

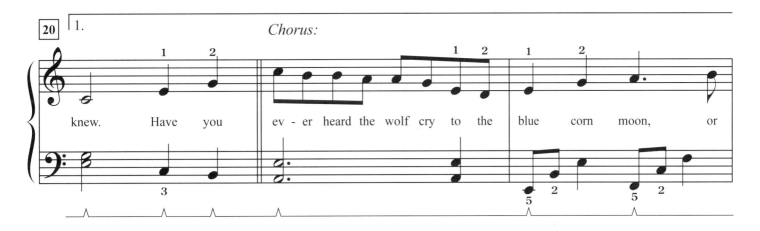

1.   *Chorus:*

knew. Have you   ev - er heard the wolf cry to the blue   corn   moon,   or

asked the grin-ning bob-cat why he grinned? Can you   sing with all the voic-es of the

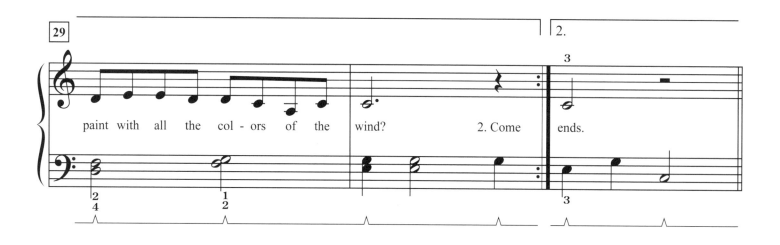

Bridge:

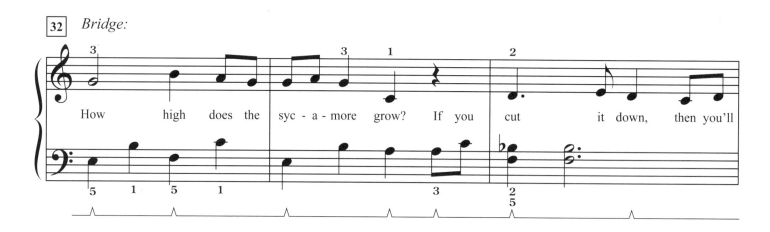

Chorus:

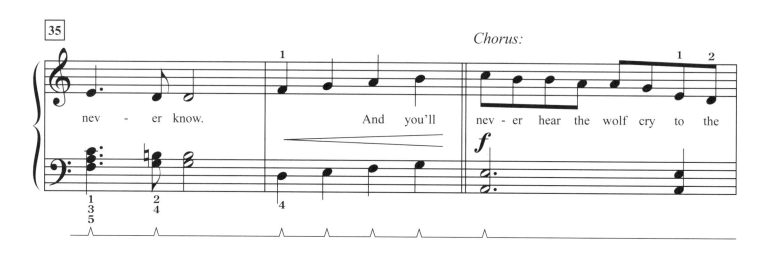

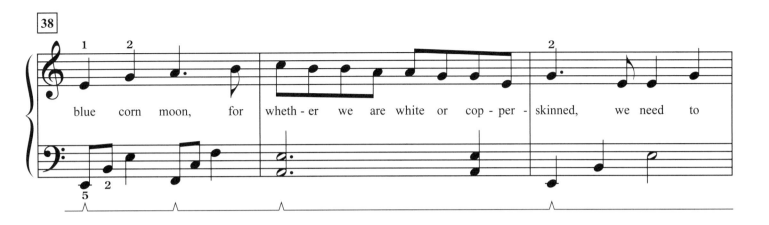

blue corn moon, for wheth - er we are white or cop - per - skinned, we need to

sing with all the voic - es of the moun - tains, need to paint with all the col - ors of the

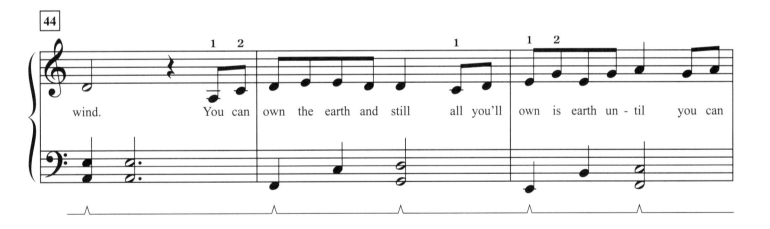

wind. You can own the earth and still all you'll own is earth un - til you can

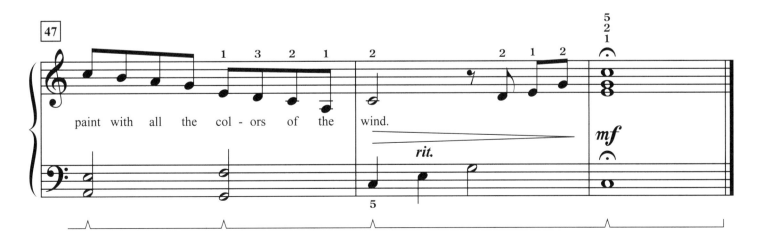

paint with all the col - ors of the wind.

rit. *mf*

Don't Stop Believin'

Words and Music by
Jonathan Cain, Neal Schon and Steve Perry
Arr. Dan Coates

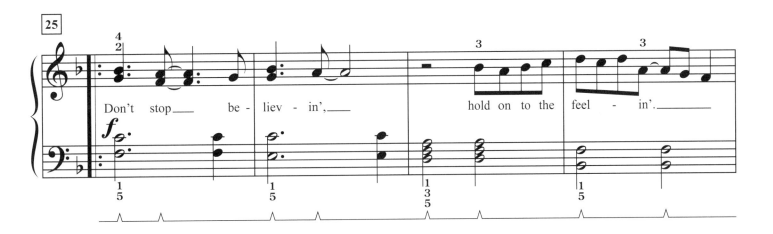

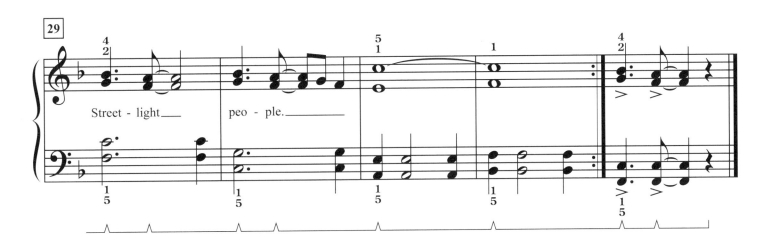

A Dream Is a Wish Your Heart Makes

(from *Cinderella*)

Words and Music by
Mack David, Al Hoffman and Jerry Livingston
Arr. Dan Coates

Slowly

some - day   your   rain - bow will come smil - ing____ through.   No mat - ter
sun - light   to find   for - tune that is smil - ing on   you.   Don't let your

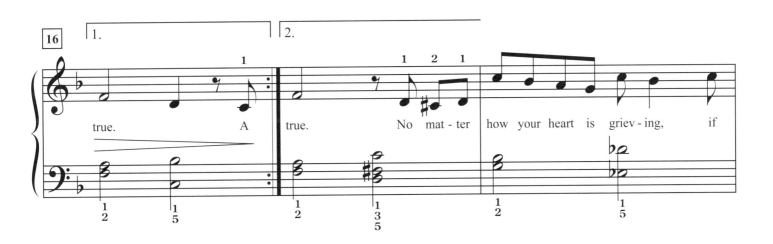

how your heart is griev - ing,   if   you keep on be - liev - ing,   the   dream that you wish   will come
heart be filled with sor - row,   for   all you know, to - mor - row   the   dream that you wish   will come

mf

_____ *simile*

1.

2.

true.   A   true.   No mat - ter   how your heart is griev - ing,   if

you keep on be - liev - ing,   the   dream   that you wish   will come   true.

mp *rit.*

Embraceable You

Music and Lyrics by
George Gershwin and Ira Gershwin
Arr. Dan Coates

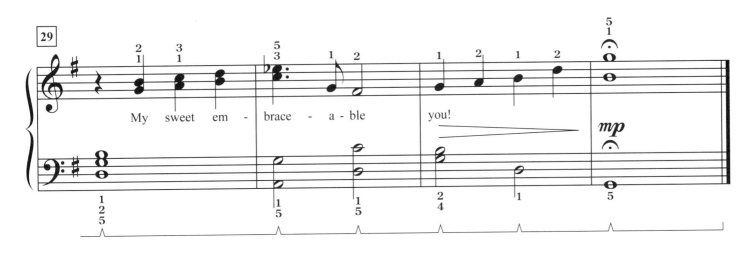

The Greatest Love of All

Words by Linda Creed
Music by Michael Masser
Arr. Dan Coates

How Do I Live

Words and Music by Diane Warren
Arr. Dan Coates

Moderately slow

Verse:

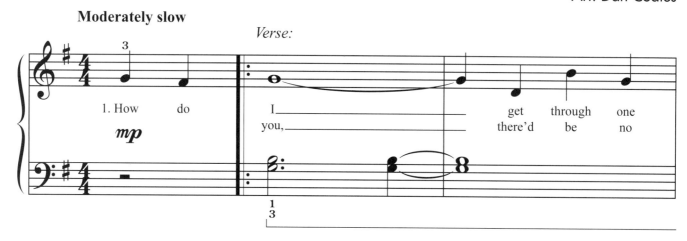

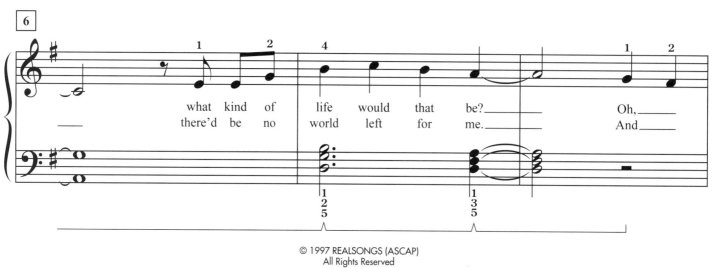

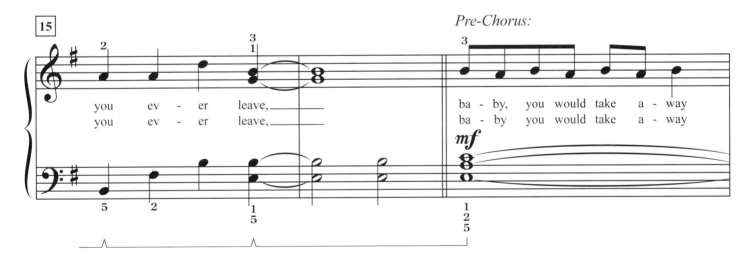

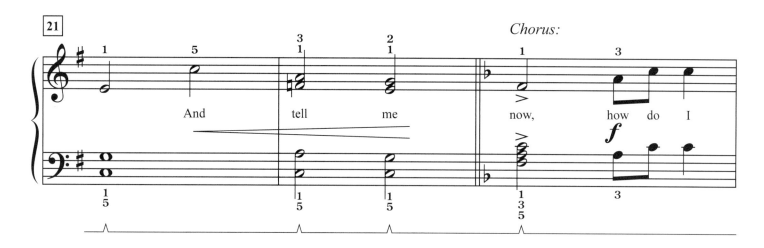

Chorus:

And tell me now, how do I

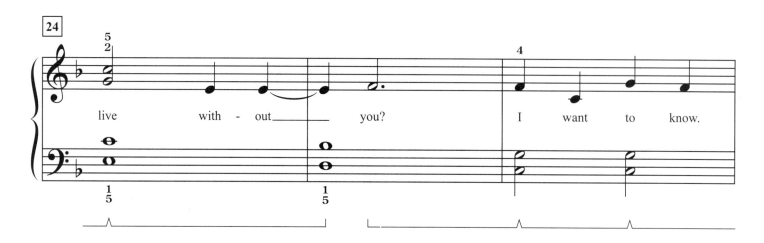

live with - out you? I want to know.

How do I breathe with - out you, if

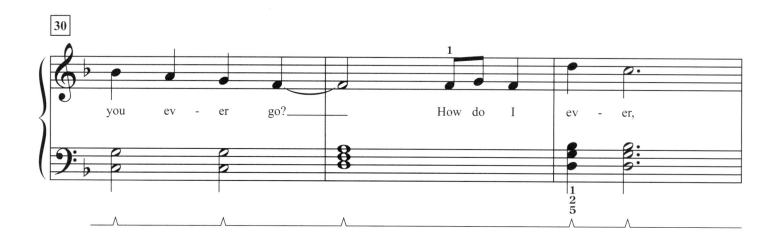

you ev - er go? How do I ev - er,

ev - er   sur - vive?   How do I,   how do I,

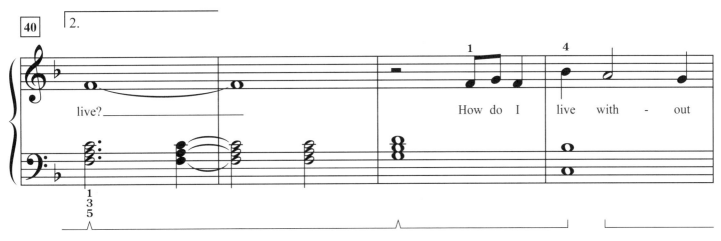

oh,   how do I   live?   2. With - out

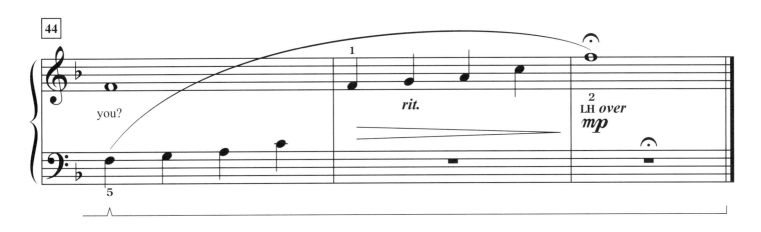

2.

live?   How do I   live   with - out

you?   rit.   LH *over*
mp

I Could Have Danced All Night

(from *My Fair Lady*)

Lyrics by Alan Jay Lerner
Music by Frederick Loewe
Arr. Dan Coates

Brightly

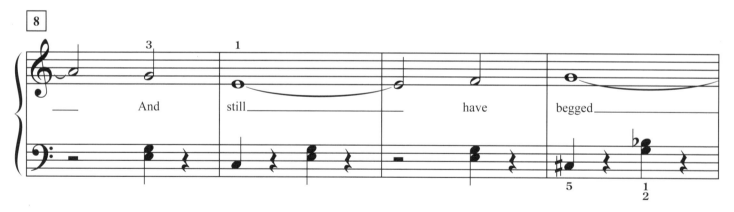

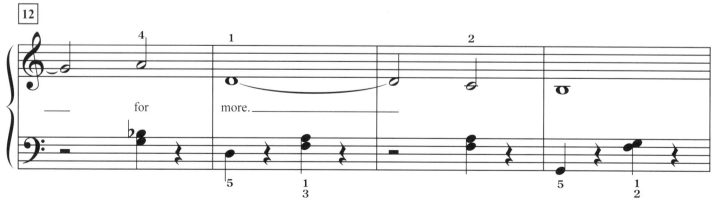

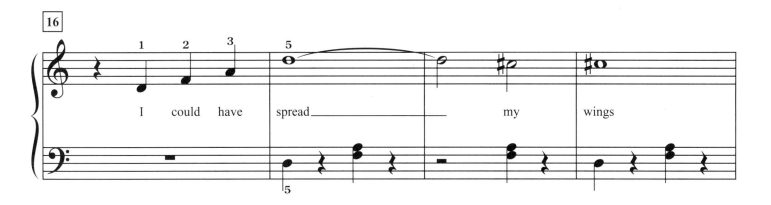

I could have spread my wings

and done a thou - sand things

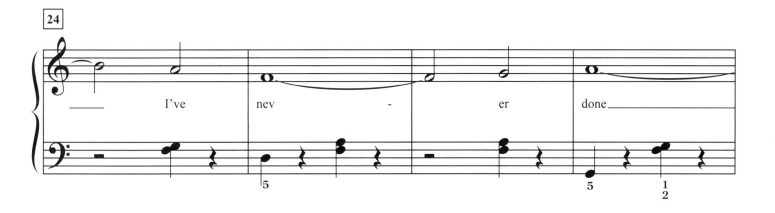

I've nev - er done

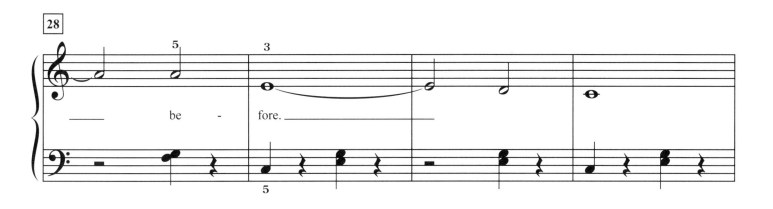

be - fore.

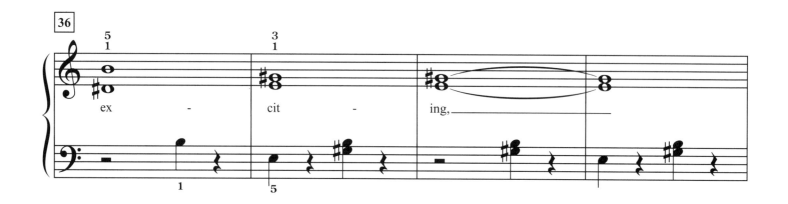

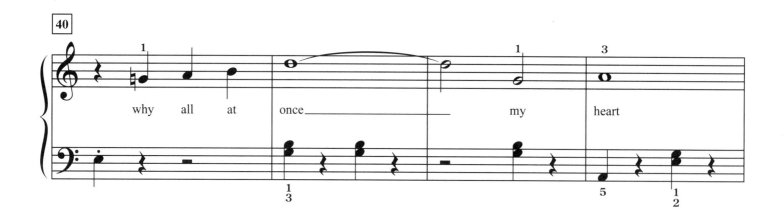

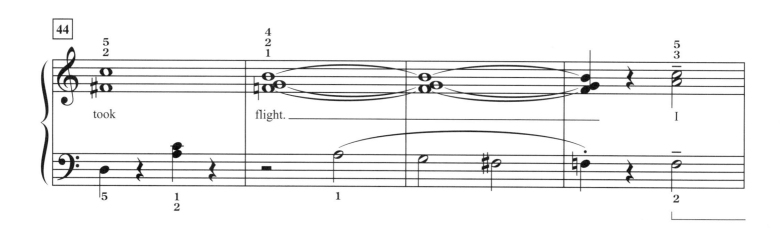

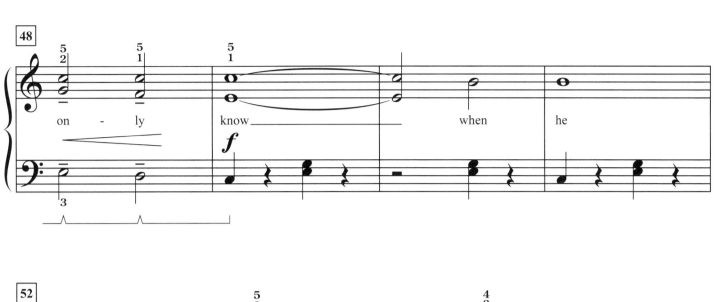

on - ly know_____ when he

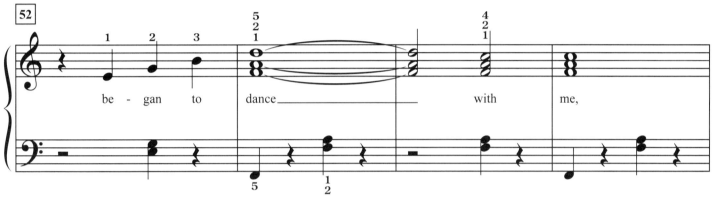

be - gan to dance_____ with me,

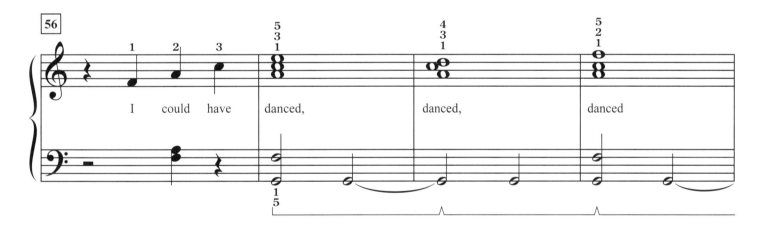

I could have danced, danced, danced

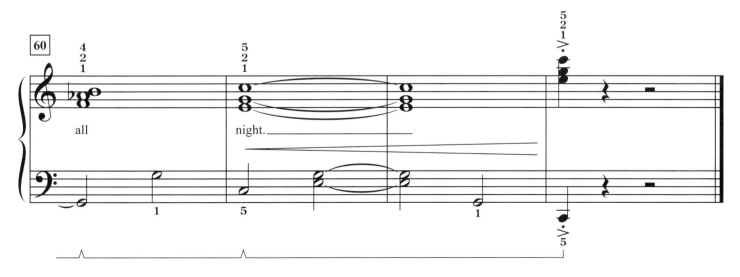

all night._____

I Got Rhythm

Music and Lyrics by
George Gershwin and Ira Gershwin
Arr. Dan Coates

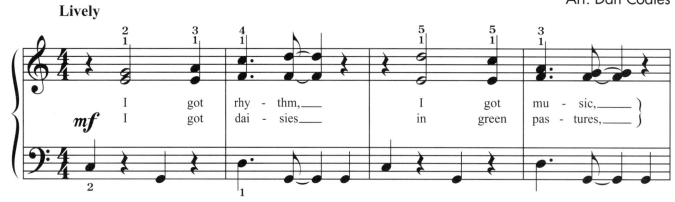

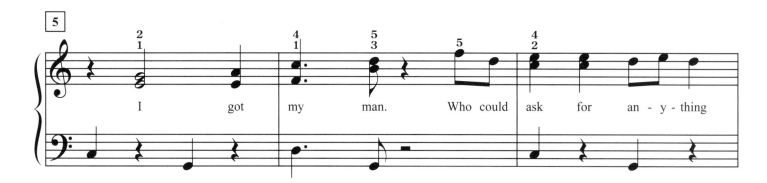

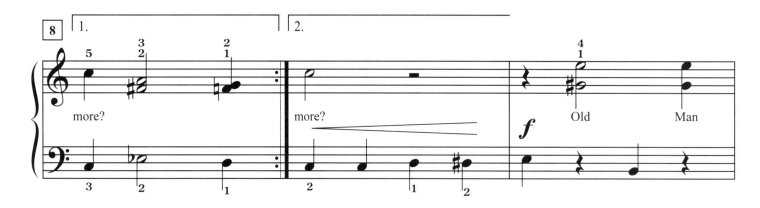

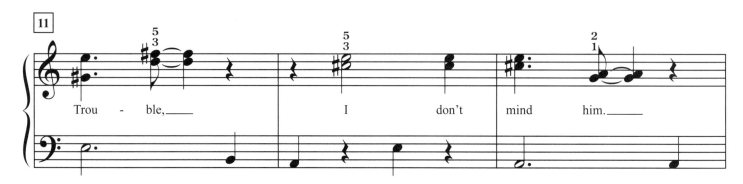

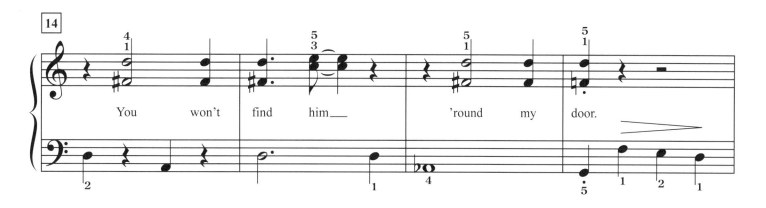

You won't find him___ 'round my door.

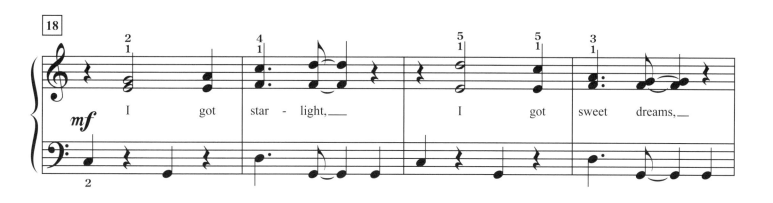

I got star - light,___ I got sweet dreams,___

I got my man, who could ask for an - y - thing

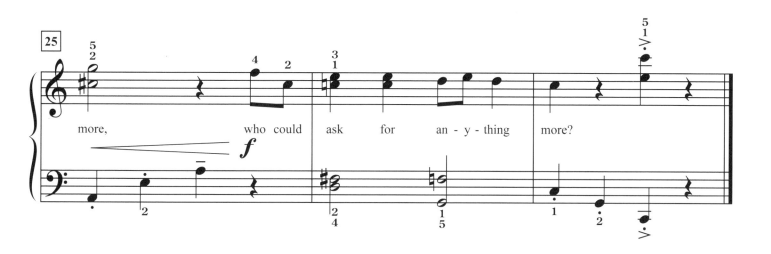

more, who could ask for an - y - thing more?

If Ever I Would Leave You

(from *Camelot*)

Music by Frederick Loewe
Lyrics by Alan Jay Lerner
Arr. Dan Coates

Slowly, with expression

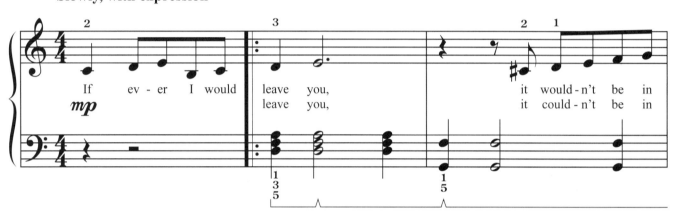

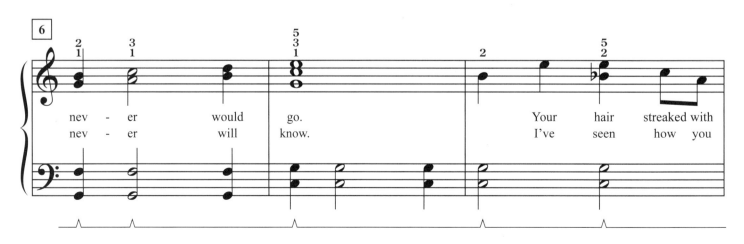

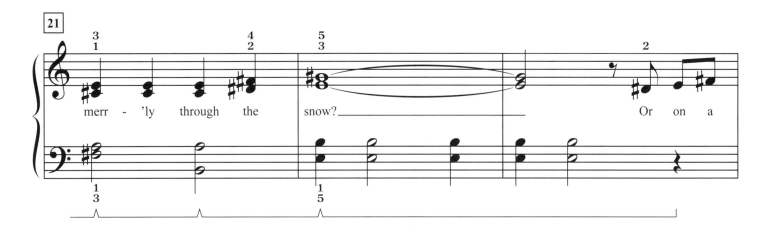

merr - 'ly through the snow?_____ Or on a

win - try eve - ning when you catch the fi - re's glow?

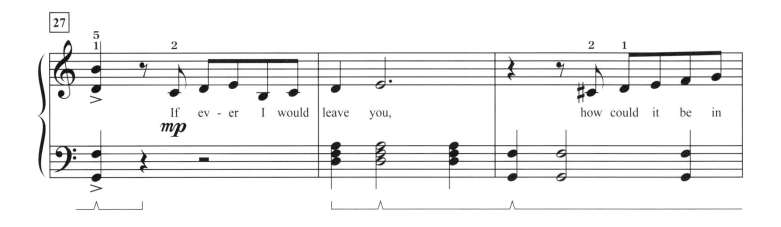

If ev - er I would leave you, how could it be in

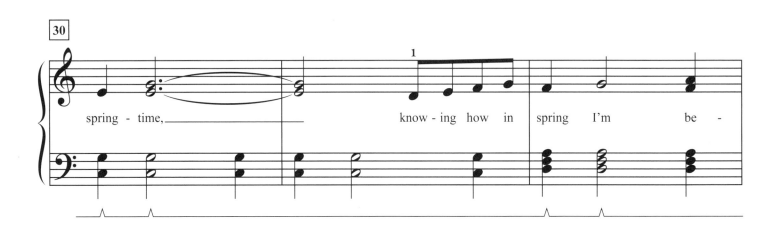

spring - time,_____ know - ing how in spring I'm be -

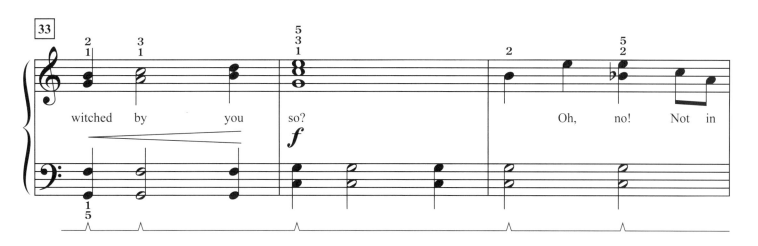

witched by   you   so?   Oh,   no!   Not   in

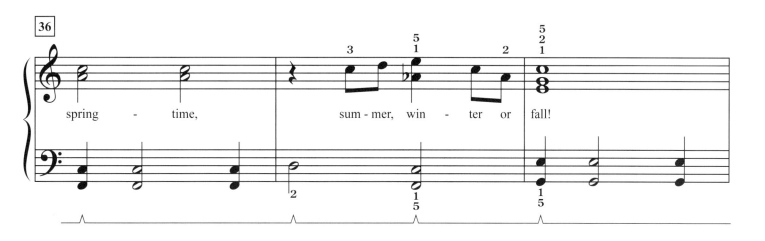

spring - time,   sum - mer,   win - ter   or   fall!

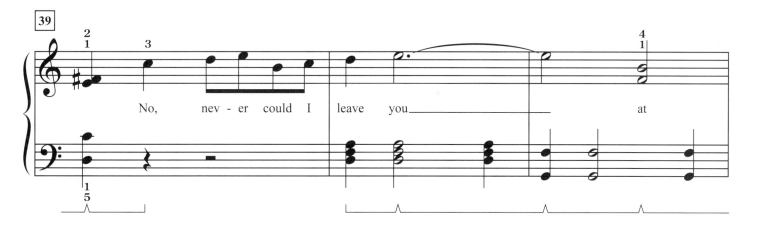

No,   nev - er   could   I   leave   you _____   at

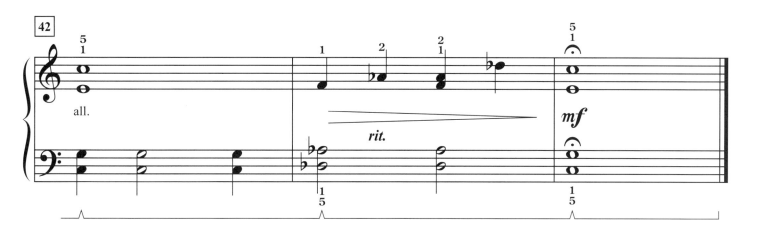

all.

If I Only Had a Brain

(from *The Wizard of Oz*)

Music by Harold Arlen
Lyrics by E.Y. Harburg
Arr. Dan Coates

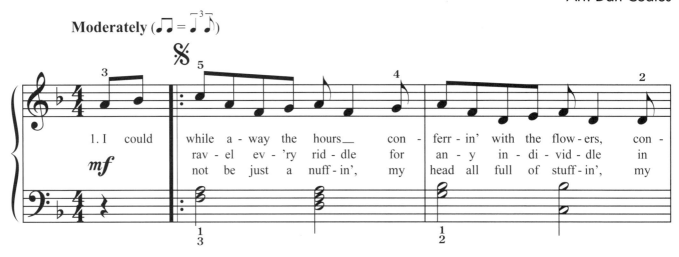

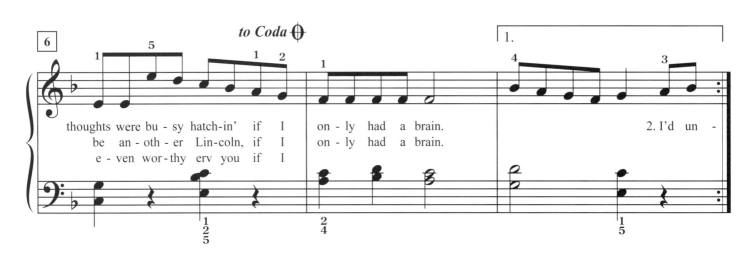

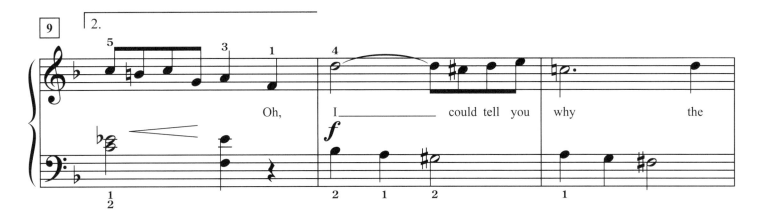

Oh, I_____ could tell you why the

o - cean's near the shore, I could think of things I nev - er thunk be -

D.S. al Coda

fore and then I'd sit and think some more. 3. I would

⊕ *Coda*

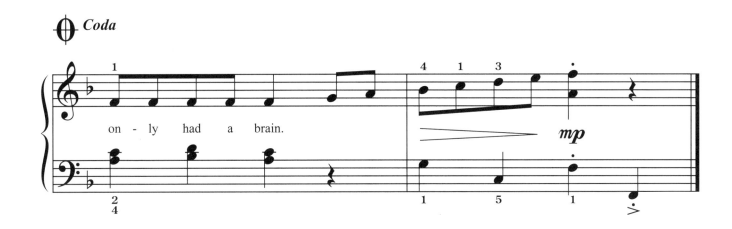

on - ly had a brain.

The Imperial March (Darth Vader's Theme)

(from *Star Wars: The Empire Strikes Back*)

Music by **JOHN WILLIAMS**
Arr. Dan Coates

Steady march

Killing Me Softly

Words and Music by
Charles Fox and Norman Gimbel
Arr. Dan Coates

Moderately slow

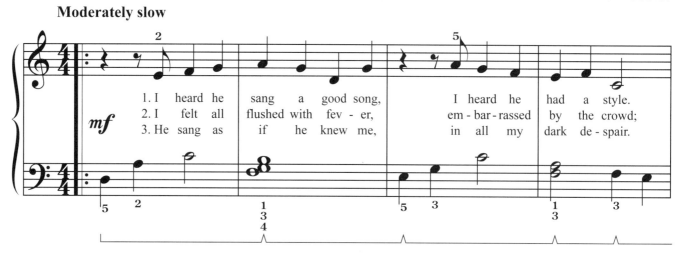

1. I heard he sang a good song, I heard he had a style.
2. I felt all flushed with fev-er, em-bar-rassed by the crowd;
3. He sang as if he knew me, in all my dark de-spair.

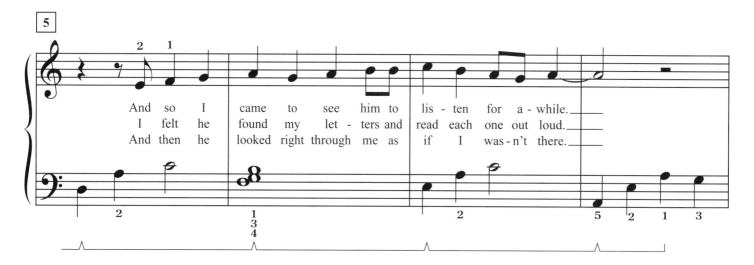

And so I came to see him to lis-ten for a-while.
I felt he found my let-ters and read each one out loud.
And then he looked right through me as if I was-n't there.

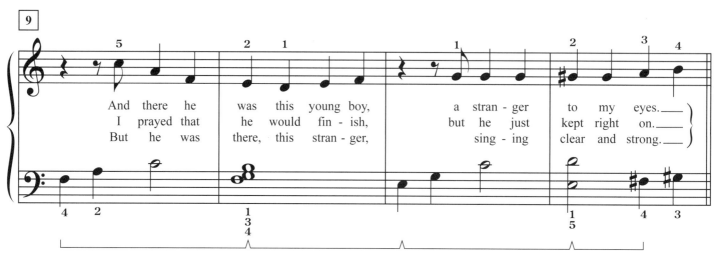

And there he was this young boy, a stran-ger to my eyes.
I prayed that he would fin-ish, but he just kept right on.
But he was there, this stran-ger, sing-ing clear and strong.

Strum-ming my pain__ with his fin - gers, sing-ing my life __ with his words.

Kill-ing me soft - ly with his song, kill-ing me soft - ly with his song. Tell-ing my

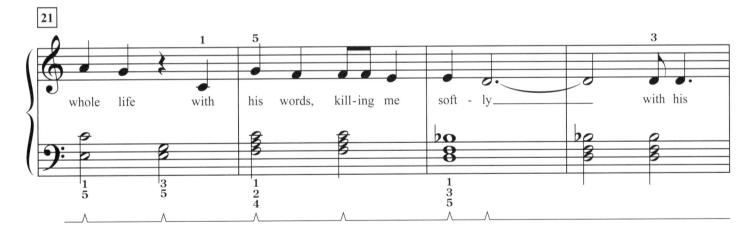

whole life with his words, kill-ing me soft - ly__ with his

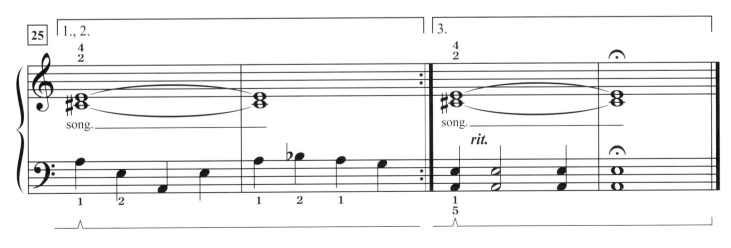

1., 2.

3.

song.__

song.__

rit.

In Dreams

(from *The Lord of the Rings: The Fellowship of the Ring*)

Words and Music by
Fran Walsh and Howard Shore
Arr. Dan Coates

Moderately slow

When the cold of win - ter comes, star - less night will cov - er

day._____ In the veil - ing of the sun we will walk in bit - ter

rain. But in dreams, I can____ hear____ your

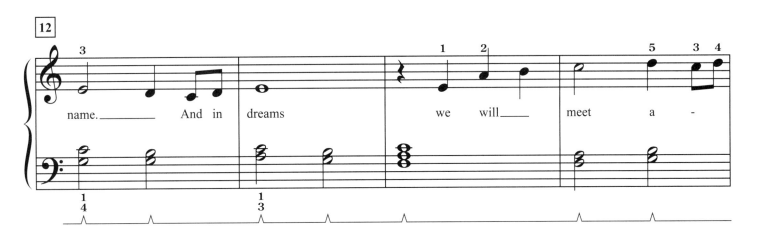

name._____ And in dreams   we will____ meet a -

gain.   When the seas and moun-tains fall   and we

come   to end of days,_____ in the dark I hear a call,   call-ing me

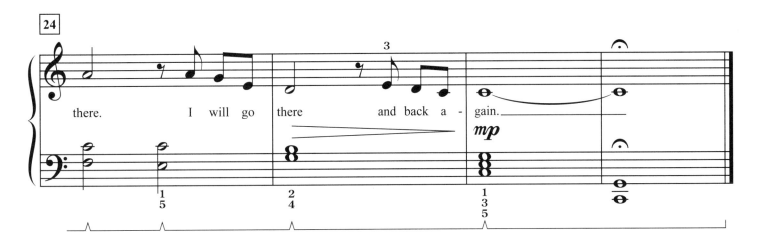

there.   I will go there   and back a - gain._____

Let It Go

(from Walt Disney's *Frozen*)

Music and Lyrics by
Kristen Anderson-Lopez and Robert Lopez
Arr. Dan Coates

13

Could-n't keep it in, heav-en knows I've tried.

17 *Pre-Chorus:*

mf

Don't let them in, don't let them see. Be the good girl you

20

al - ways have to be. Con - ceal, don't feel, don't let them know.

23

Well, now they know. Let it go,

let it go. _____ I am one _____ with the wind _____ and sky. _____ Let it go,

_____ let it go. You'll nev - er see _____ me _____ cry. _____

Here I _____ stand, _____ _____ and here I'll _____ stay. _____ Let the

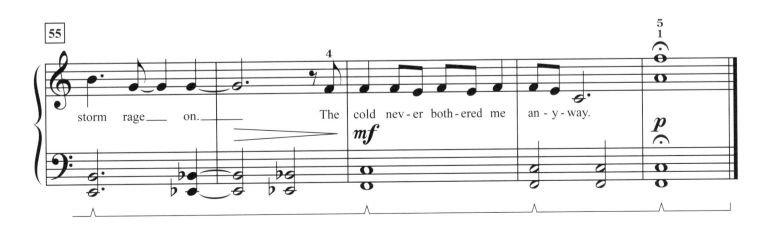

storm rage _____ on. _____ _____ The cold nev - er both - ered me an - y - way.

mf   *p*

Misty

Words by Johnny Burke
Music by Erroll Garner
Arr. Dan Coates

hand.   Walk my   near.

You   can   say   that   you're   lead - ing   me   on,

but it's just what I want you to do.   Don't you no - tice how

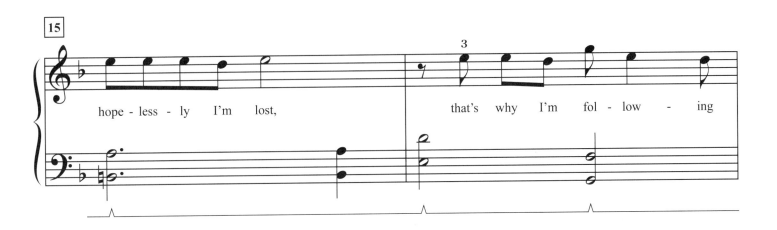

hope - less - ly I'm lost,   that's why I'm fol - low - ing

you.   On my own,   would I

wan - der through this won - der - land a - lone,   nev - er know - ing my

right foot from my left,   my   hat_____ from my glove,_____ I'm too

mist - y   and too much in   love.   *rit.*   *mp*

My Funny Valentine

Words by Lorenz Hart
Music by Richard Rodgers
Arr. Dan Coates

Slowly, with expression

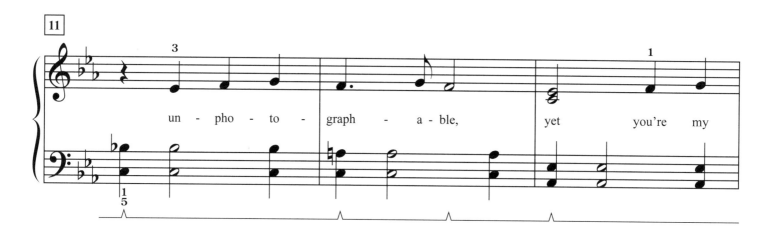

un - pho - to - graph - a - ble, yet you're my

fav - 'rite work of art. Is your

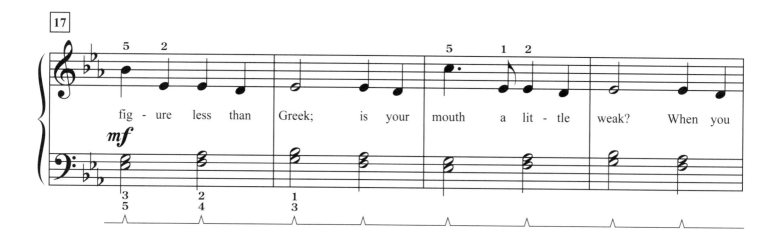

fig - ure less than Greek; is your mouth a lit - tle weak? When you

mf

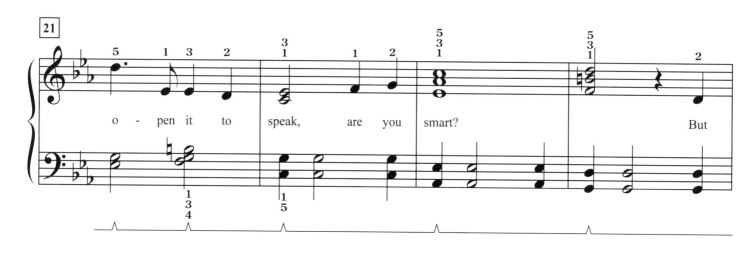

o - pen it to speak, are you smart? But

The Notebook

Written by Aaron Zigman
Arr. Dan Coates

Slowly, with expression

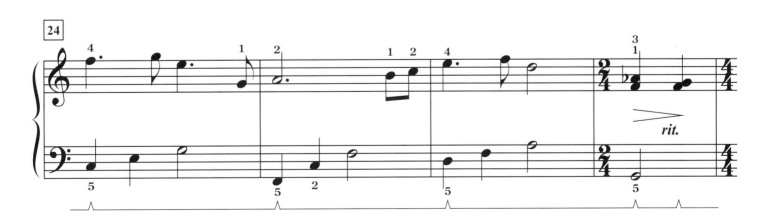

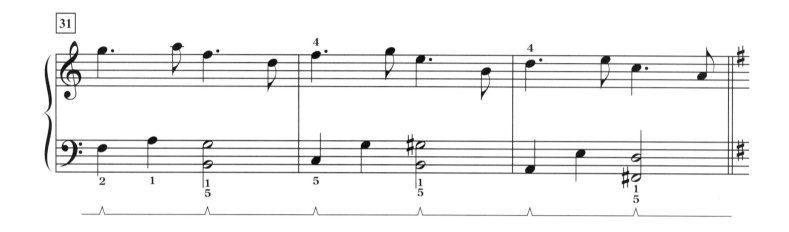

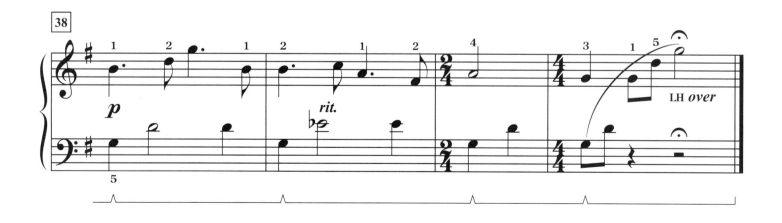

Open Arms

Words and Music by
Jonathan Cain and Steve Perry
Arr. Dan Coates

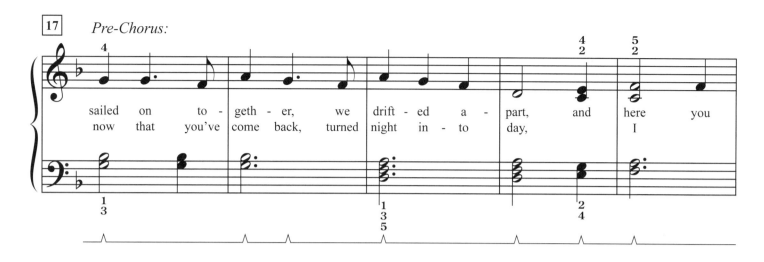

17 *Pre-Chorus:*

sailed on to - geth - er, we drift - ed a - part, and here you
now that you've come back, turned night in - to day, I

22

are by my side.
need you to stay.

So now I

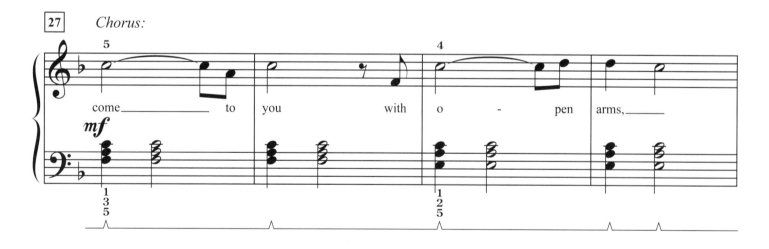

27 *Chorus:*

come_____ to you with o - pen arms,_____

mf

31

noth - ing to hide, be - lieve what I say. So

Over the Rainbow

(from *The Wizard of Oz*)

Music by Harold Arlen
Lyrics by E.Y. Harburg
Arr. Dan Coates

Moderately, with expression

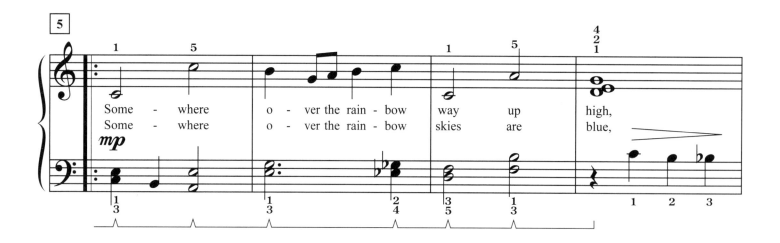

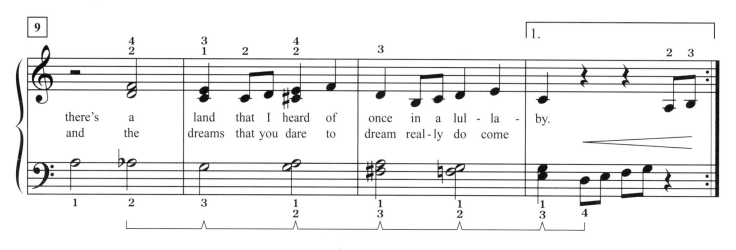

true. Some - day I'll wish up - on a star and wake up where the clouds are far be -

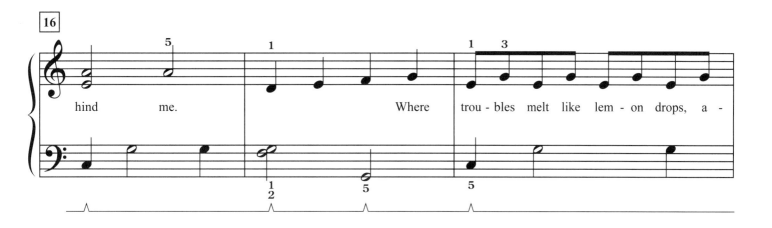

hind me. Where trou - bles melt like lem - on drops, a -

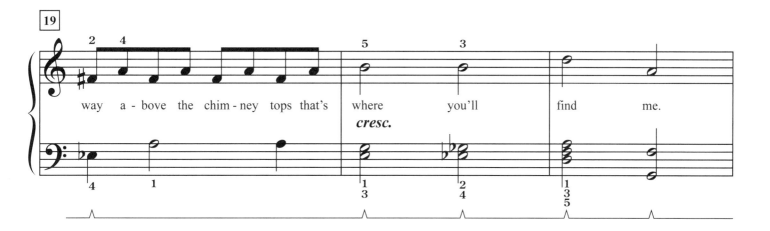

way a - bove the chim - ney tops that's where you'll find me.

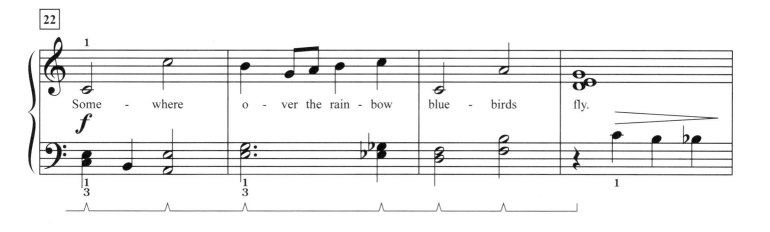

Some - where o - ver the rain - bow blue - birds fly.

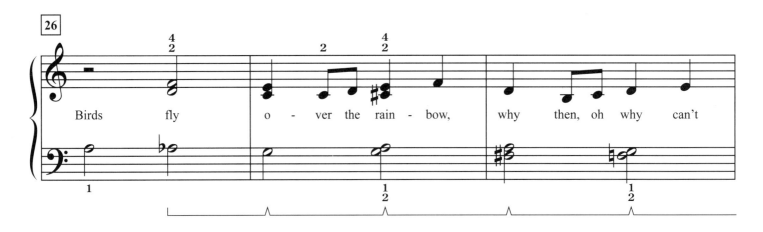

Birds fly o - ver the rain - bow, why then, oh why can't

I?

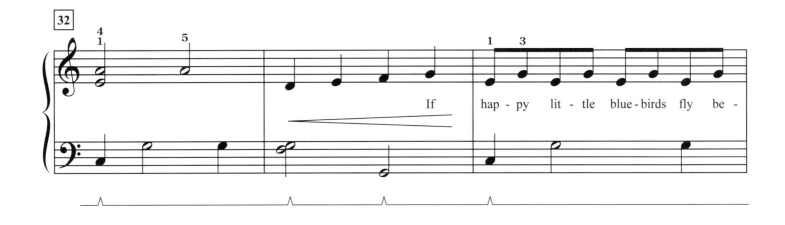

If hap - py lit - tle blue - birds fly be -

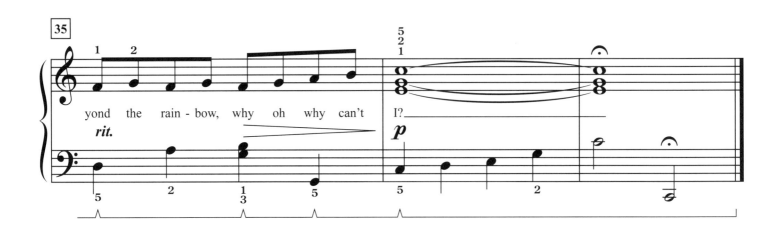

yond the rain - bow, why oh why can't I?

People

(from *Funny Girl*)

Words by Bob Merrill
Music by Jule Styne
Arr. Dan Coates

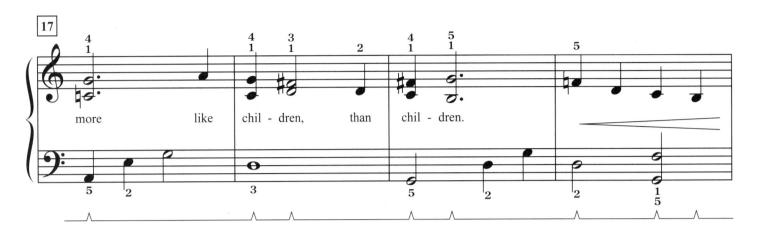

more like chil - dren, than chil - dren.

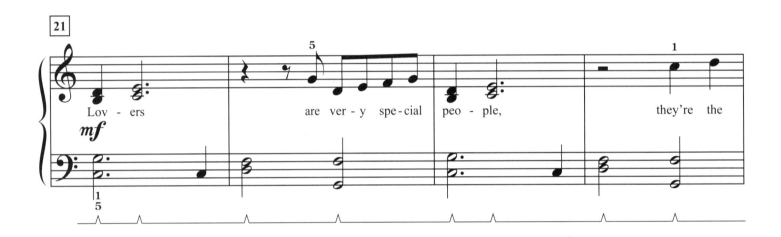

Lov - ers _mf_ are ver - y spe - cial peo - ple, they're the

luck - i - est peo - ple _ in the world. With one

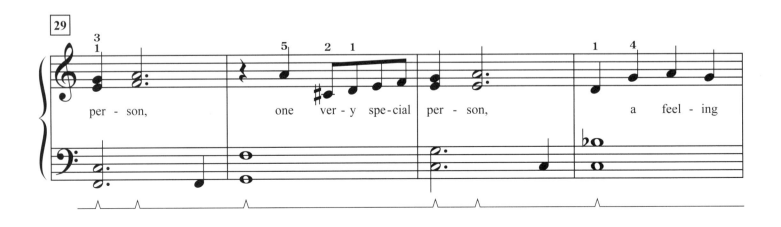

per - son, one ver - y spe - cial per - son, a feel - ing

deep in your soul says you were half, now you're whole. No more

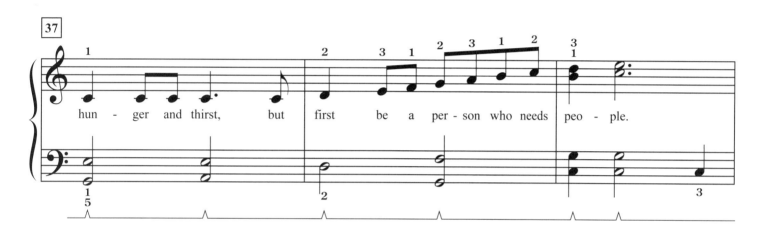

hun - ger and thirst, but first be a per - son who needs peo - ple.

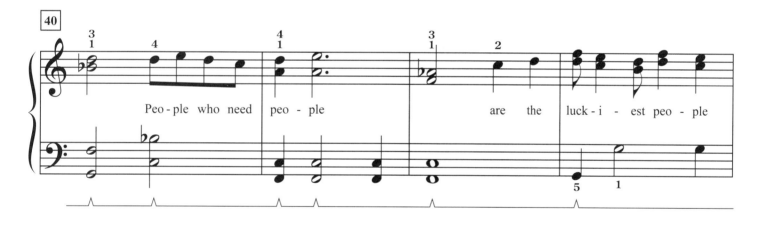

Peo - ple who need peo - ple are the luck - i - est peo - ple

in the world.

rit. *f*

The Prayer

Words and Music by
Carole Bayer Sager and David Foster
Arr. Dan Coates

Slowly, with expression

The Pink Panther

By Henry Mancini
Arr. Dan Coates

Mysteriously

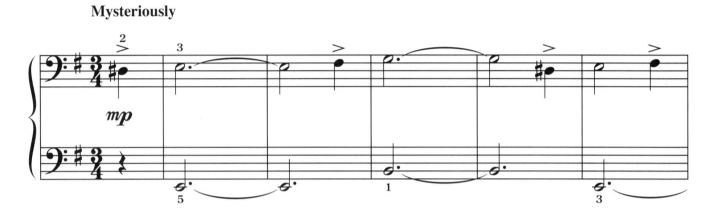

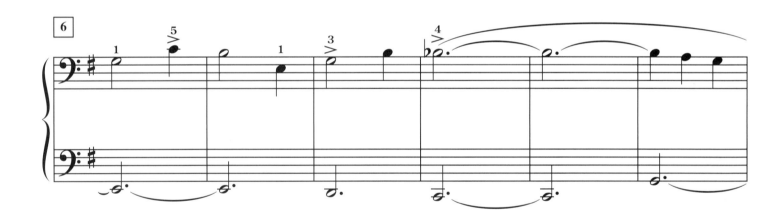

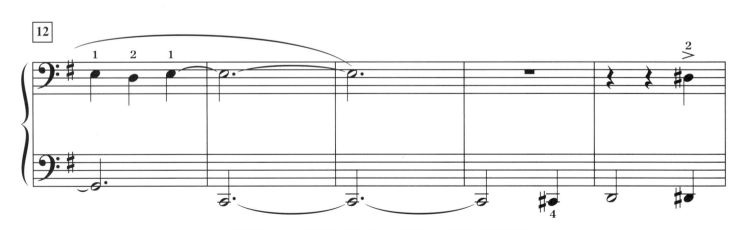

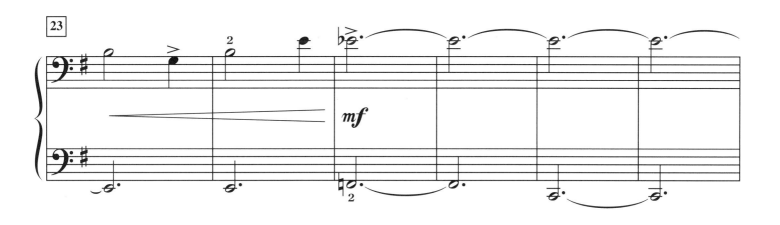

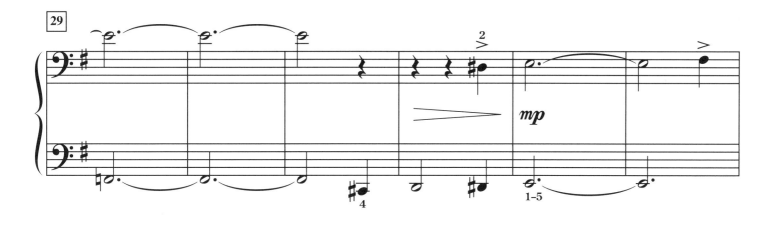

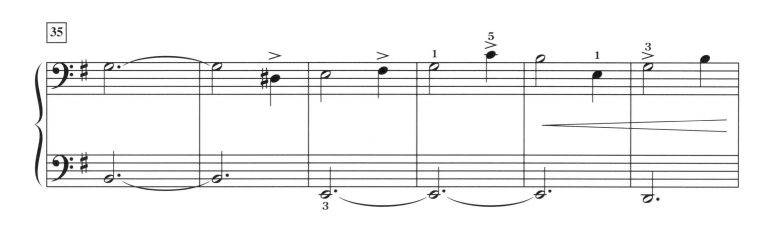

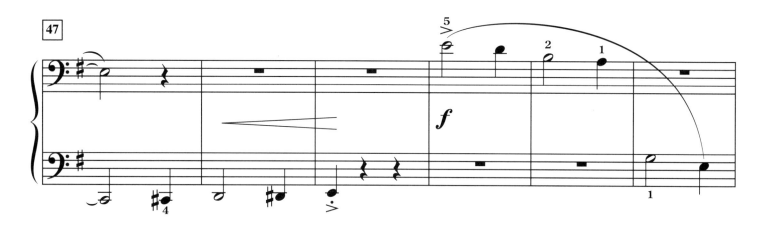

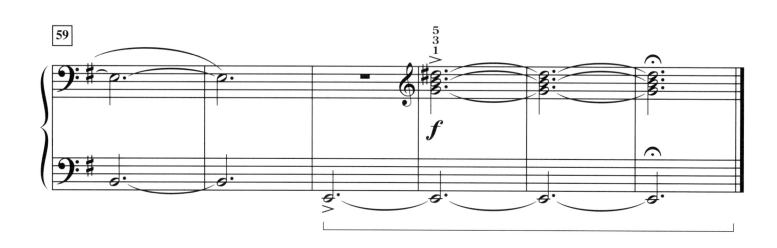

Someone to Watch Over Me

Music and Lyrics by
George Gershwin and Ira Gershwin
Arr. Dan Coates

Moderately slow

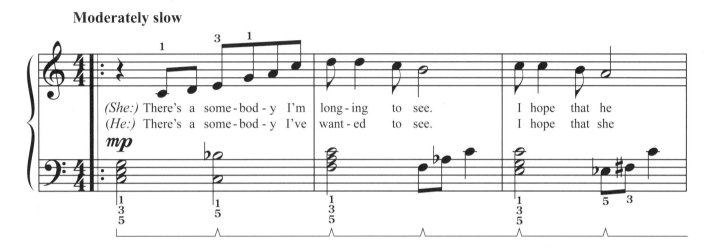

(She:) There's a some-bod-y I'm long-ing to see. I hope that he
(He:) There's a some-bod-y I've want-ed to see. I hope that she

turns out to be some - one who'll watch o - ver
turns out to be some - one who'll watch o - ver

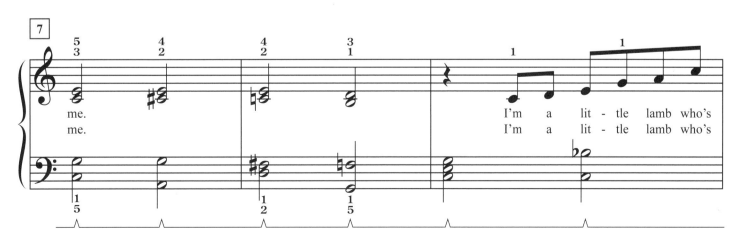

me. I'm a lit - tle lamb who's
me. I'm a lit - tle lamb who's

Singin' in the Rain

(from *Singin' in the Rain*)

Music by Nacio Herb Brown
Lyric by Arthur Freed
Arr. Dan Coates

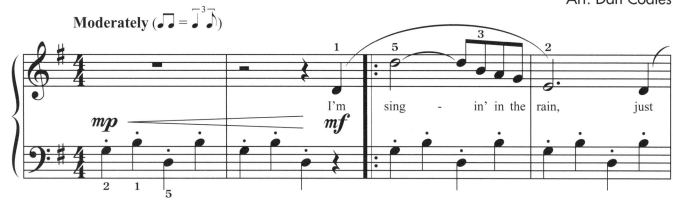

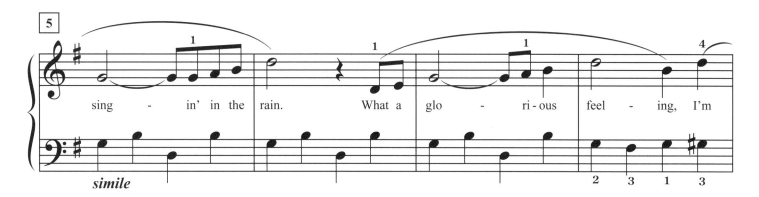

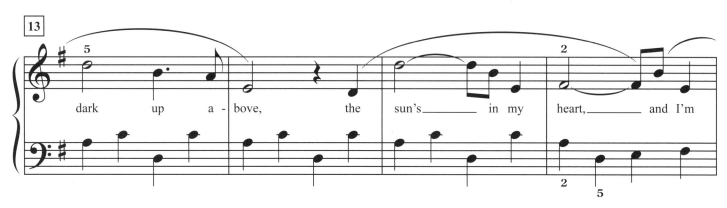

Stairway to Heaven

Words and Music by
Jimmy Page and Robert Plant
Arr. Dan Coates

10

There's a

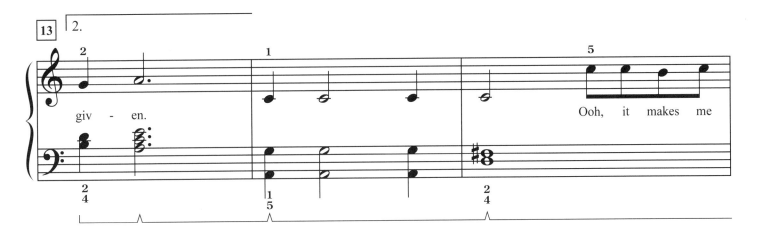

13

2.

giv - en.

Ooh, it makes me

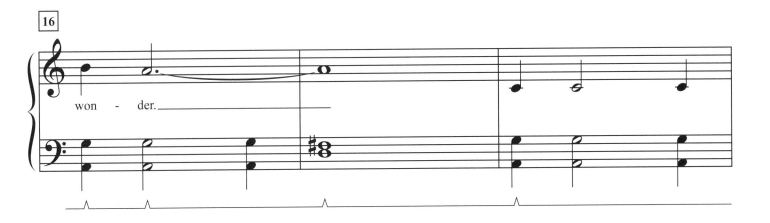

16

won - der. ___

19

It makes me won - der.

There's a

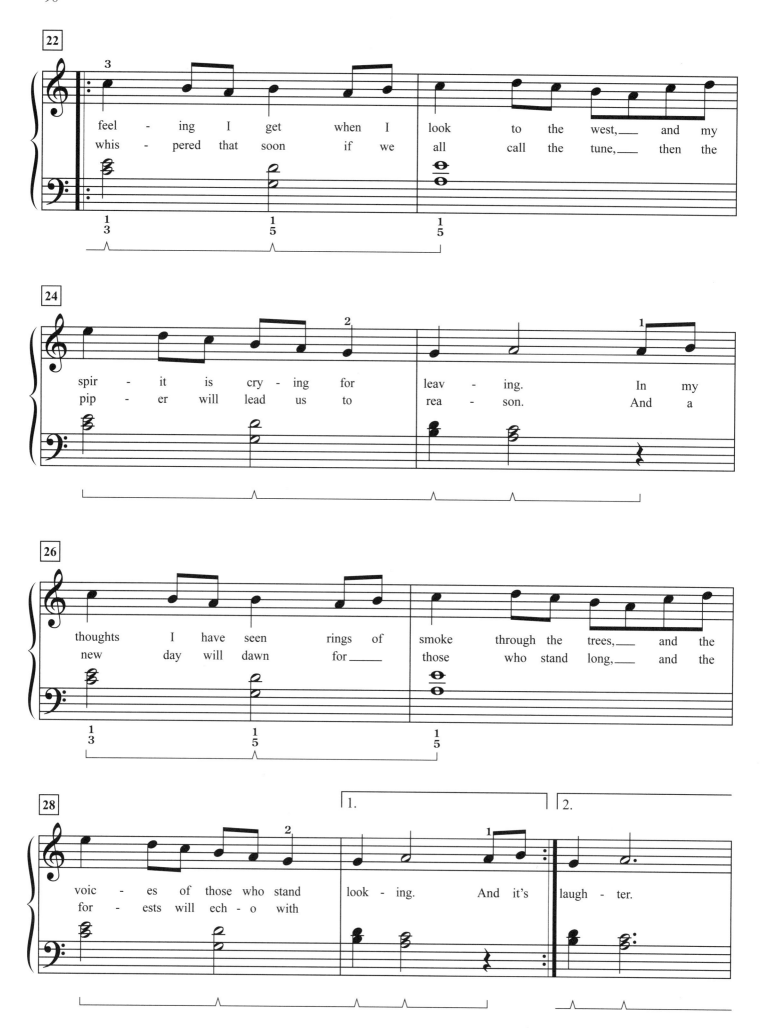

With a steady beat

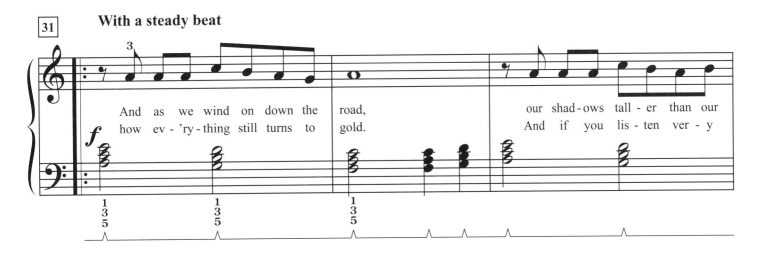

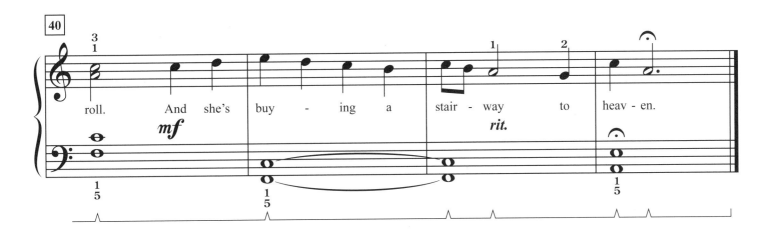

Star Wars

(Main Theme)

Music by **JOHN WILLIAMS**
Arr. Dan Coates

Majestically

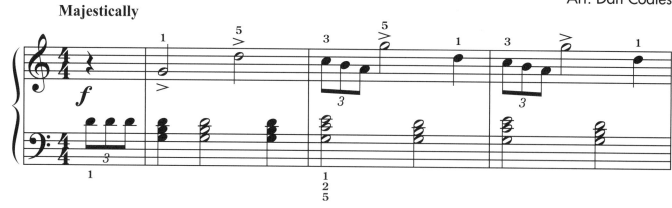

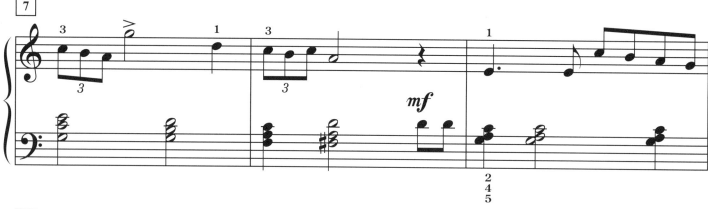

They Can't Take That Away from Me

Music and Lyrics by
George Gershwin and Ira Gershwin
Arr. Dan Coates

the way you haunt my dreams, no, no, they

can't take that a - way from me! We may nev - er, nev - er

meet a - gain on the bump - y road to love. Still I'll

al - ways, al - ways keep the mem - r'y of...

The way you hold your knife, the way we danced till

three, the way you've changed my life,

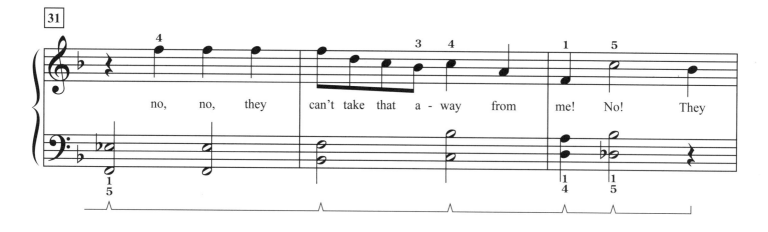

no, no, they can't take that a-way from me! No! They

can't take that a-way from me.

Tomorrow

(from *Annie*)

Music by Charles Strouse
Lyric by Martin Charnin
Arr. Dan Coates

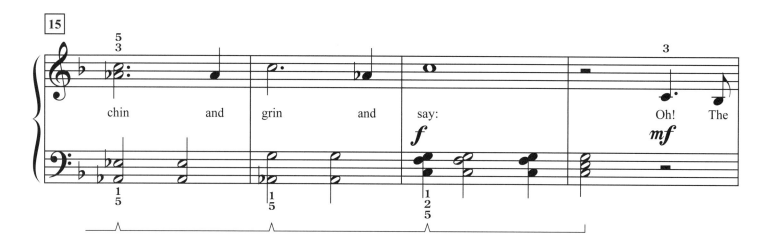

chin and grin and say: Oh! The

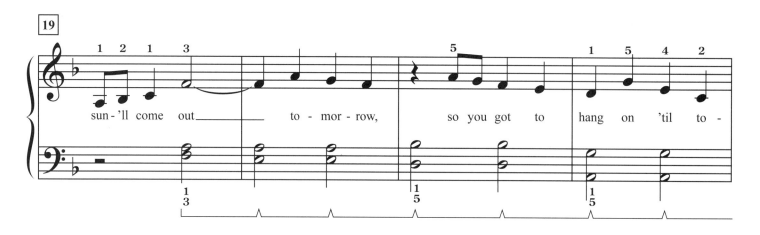

sun-'ll come out____ to-mor-row, so you got to hang on 'til to-

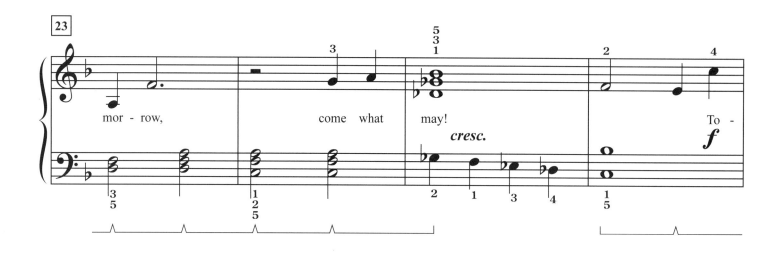

mor-row, come what may! To-

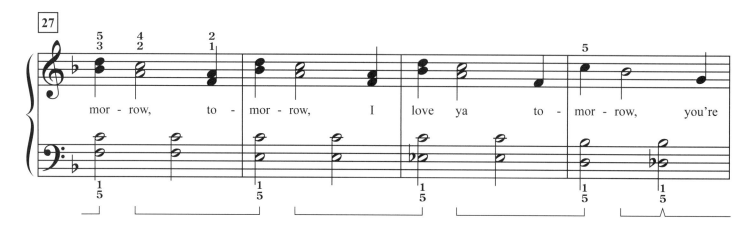

mor-row, to-mor-row, I love ya to-mor-row, you're

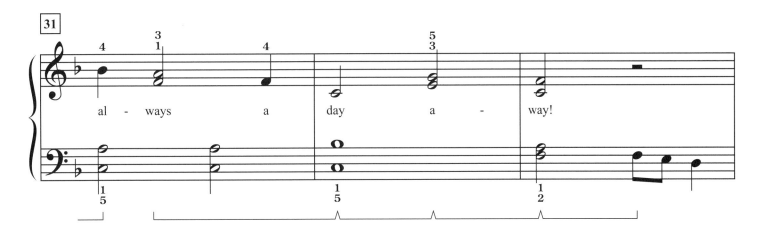

al - ways a day a - way!

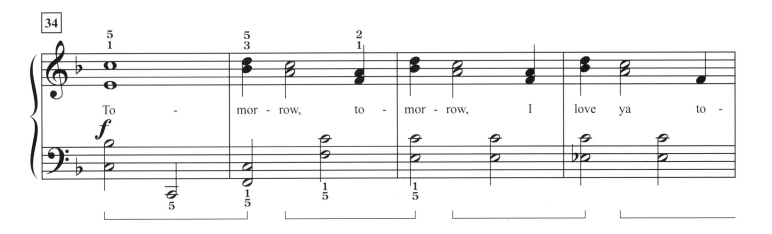

To - mor - row, to - mor - row, I love ya to -

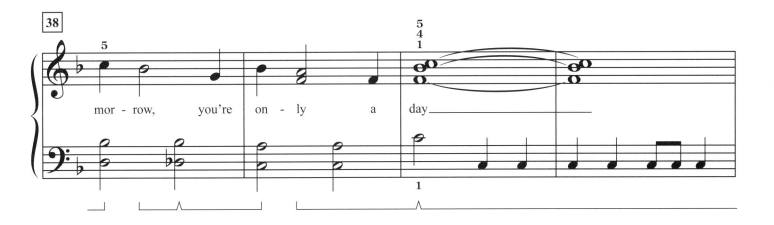

mor - row, you're on - ly a day

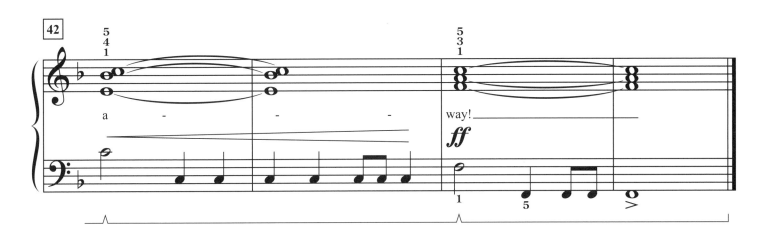

a - - - - way!

Try to Remember

(from *The Fantasticks*)

Lyrics by Tom Jones
Music by Harvey Schmidt
Arr. Dan Coates

Slowly, with tenderness

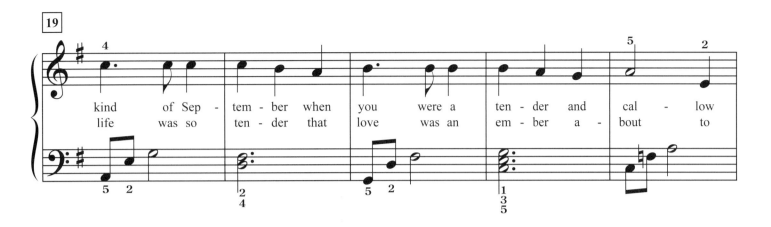

kind of Sep - tem - ber when you were a ten - der and cal - low
life was so ten - der that love was an em - ber a - bout to

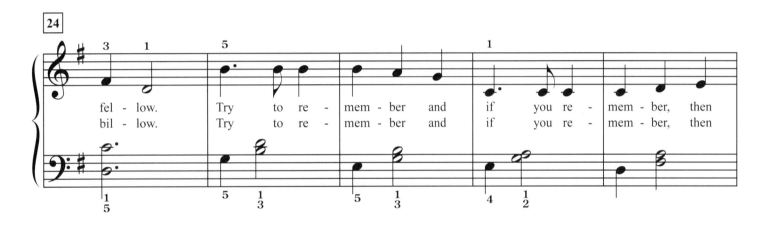

fel - low. Try to re - mem - ber and if you re - mem - ber, then
bil - low. Try to re - mem - ber and if you re - mem - ber, then

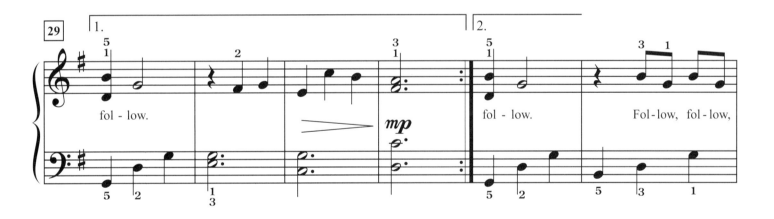

1.

fol - low.

mp

2.

fol - low. Fol-low, fol-low,

fol-low, fol-low, fol-low, fol-low, fol-low, fol-low, fol - low.

rit. *p*

Un-break My Heart

Words and Music by Diane Warren
Arr. Dan Coates

Moderately slow

Verse:

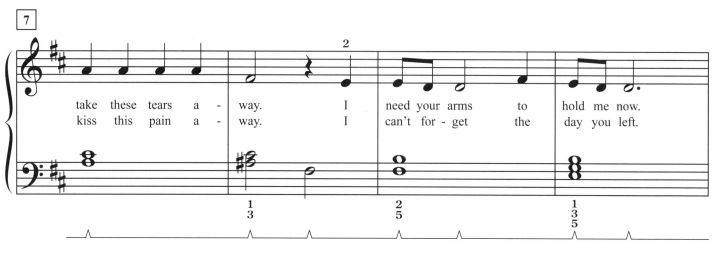

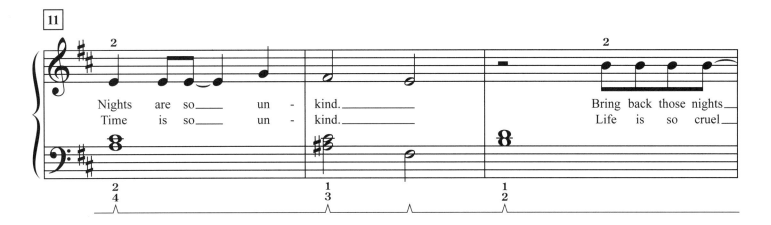

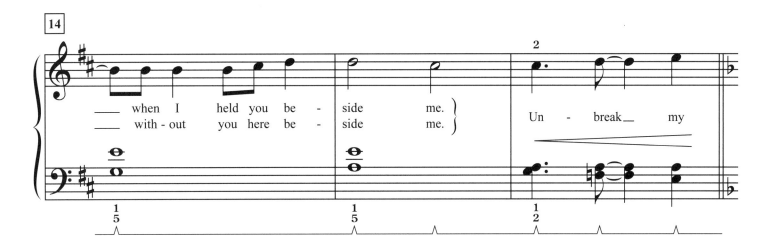

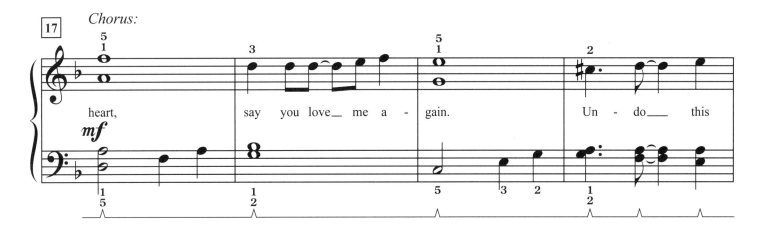

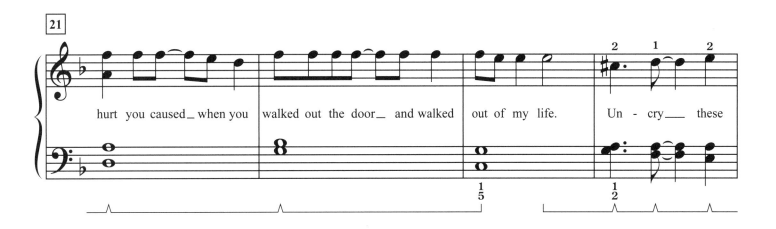

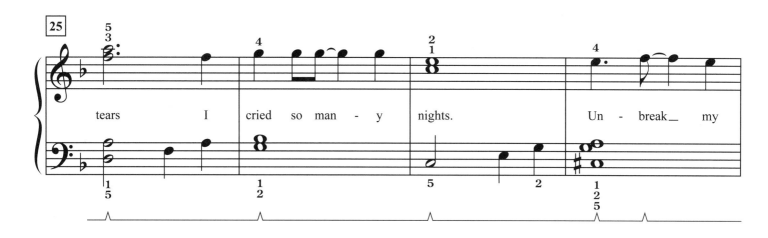

tears I cried so man - y nights. Un - break __ my

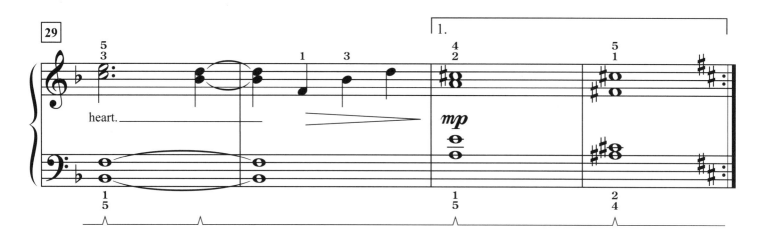

heart. __

Un - break __ my heart.

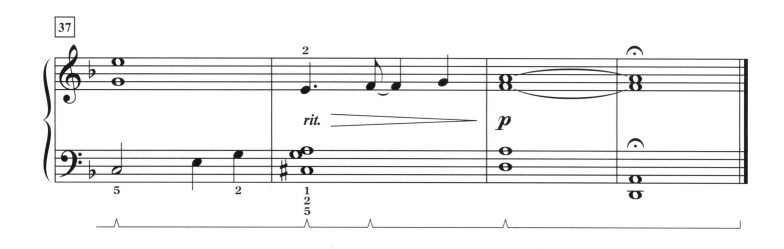

rit. p

A Whole New World

(from Walt Disney's *Aladdin*)

Words by Tim Rice
Music by Alan Menken
Arr. Dan Coates

Moderately, steady

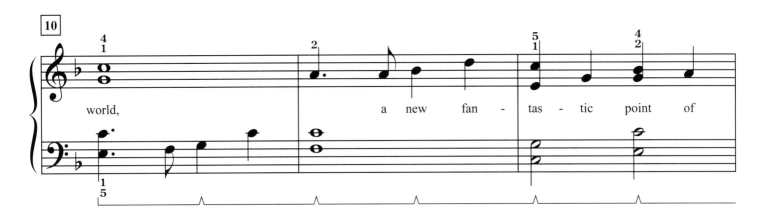

world, a new fan - tas - tic point of

view. No one to tell us no or where to go or

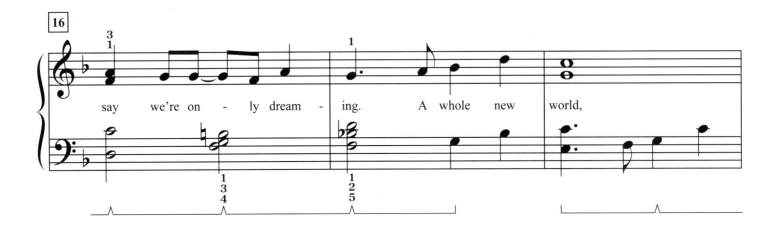

say we're on - ly dream - ing. A whole new world,

a daz - zling place I nev - er knew. But when I'm

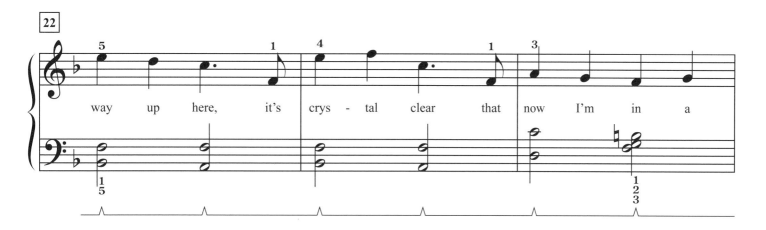

way up here, it's crys - tal clear that now I'm in a

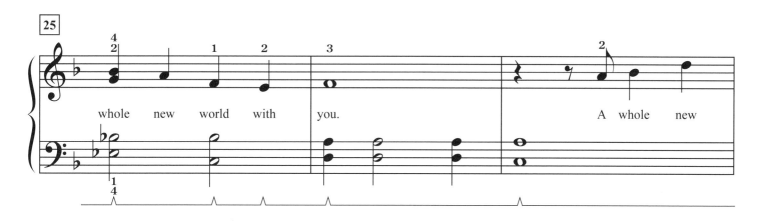

whole new world with you. A whole new

world,_____ that's where we'll be._____ A thrill - ing

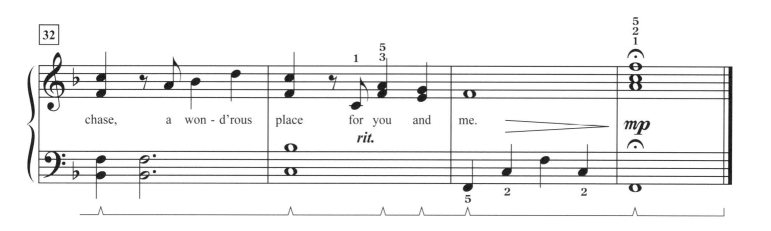

chase, a won - d'rous place for you and me.

rit. *mp*

You Raise Me Up

Words and Music by
Rolf Lovland and Brendan Graham
Arr. Dan Coates

The Wind Beneath My Wings

(from *Beaches*)

Words and Music by
Larry Henley and Jeff Silbar
Arr. Dan Coates

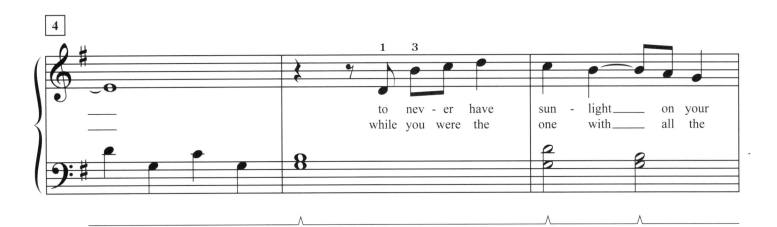

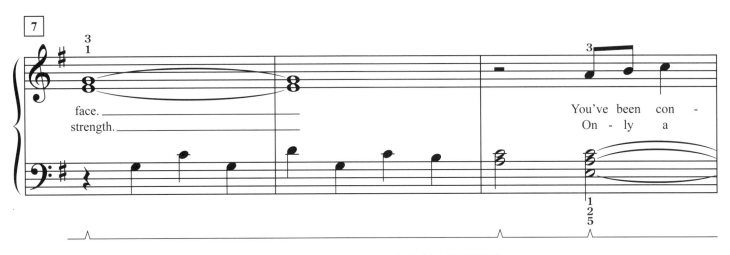